APOLLO IN THE GRASS

ALEKSANDR KUSHNER

Apollo in the Grass

SELECTED POEMS

TRANSLATED FROM THE

RUSSIAN BY CAROL UELAND

AND ROBERT CARNEVALE

FARRAR STRAUS GIROUX

NEW YORK

Farrar, Straus and Giroux

18 West 18th Street, New York 10011

Translation and Introduction copyright © 2015
by Carol Ueland and Robert Carnevale

All rights reserved

Printed in the United States of America

Published simultaneously in hardcover and paperback

First edition, 2015

Library of Congress Cataloging-in-Publication Data

Kushner, Aleksandr, author.

[Poems. Selections. English]

Apollo in the grass : selected poems / Aleksandr Kushner ;

translated from the Russian by Carol Ueland and Robert Carnevale.

pages ; cm

Includes bibliographical references.

ISBN 978-0-374-10573-0 (hardcover) — ISBN 978-0-374-53548-3 (pbk.) —
ISBN 978-0-374-71394-2 (e-book)

I. Ueland, Carol, translator. II. Carnevale, Robert, translator. III. Title.

PG3482.8.U73 A2 2015

891.71'44—dc23

2014044642

Designed by Quemadura

Farrar, Straus and Giroux books may be purchased for
educational, business, or promotional use. For information
on bulk purchases, please contact the Macmillan Corporate
and Premium Sales Department at 1-800-221-7945,
extension 5442, or write to specialmarkets@macmillan.com.

www.fsgbooks.com
www.twitter.com/fsgbooks
www.facebook.com/fsgbooks

1 3 5 7 9 10 8 6 4 2

CONTENTS

Translators' Introduction

xi

1 9 8 8 – 1 9 9 6

APOLLO IN THE GRASS

3

"These days, it would be boring, to be in London, to be in Paris"

5

"Nothing brings death closer for us"

6

"What is music?—I do not know"

7

"I know you, know you, have you down pat, I live in your heart"

9

"Give, oh give me the purple slippers with an upgathered toe"

1 0

"You will fall asleep with a lip bitten raw"

1 2

"You, soul, *entelecheia*, as you were called"

1 3

"This young Rembrandt, with his feline whiskers"

14

"There where it's Spring, Spring, always Spring"

15

"Dear Aleksandr, here where I write from, we have neither"

16

"The only thing better than Delft in
this world is this Delft on canvas"

18

"It is frightening to live and, by the same token"

20

"I am mistaken to say that poems take"

21

"I think I know where the anguished note comes from"

22

THE WATERFALL

23

"We used to write happy verses"

24

TROY

25

"In despair or in trouble, trouble"

26

1997 – 2004

"If I had been born in Germany in the same year"

29

"Do not inquire of God: He is not in this world"

30

"Poems are anachronisms. And soon they'll disappear"

31

"On seeing that cottage where you and I lived"

32

"If the city of Peter had been established on the Black Sea"

33

THE SUGARBOWL

34

LETTERS

35

"Riding into the city, you see the warehouses"

37

"I must think this through to conclusion"

39

"Whether I believe in God or do not believe in god"

40

"Maybe this life is all one poem"

41

FAREWELL TO THE CENTURY

42

"I looked at the poet and thought: it's a good thing"

44

"Here's what I envy: Prussian blue"

45

"When, in the end, that teacher in Poland"

47

VENICE

48

BUSHES

50

A PHOTOGRAPH

51

2005 – 2010

"Evening dark brought down to nothing"

57

"Having overcome barriers, rises, and steps"

58

STATUE

59

"The garden's freshness was there in the room"

6 0

"Vesuvius preserved these frescoes for us"

6 1

"I burned a small hole in my pants—above the knee"

6 2

"In the first century everything was supposed to end"

6 3

"Can you imagine what sort of poet"

6 4

"Shakespeare was mistaken to suppose"

6 6

A LITTLE PICTURE MADE FROM BLOCKS

6 7

"I was standing in front of the best equestrian statue"

6 8

FOR ONE BORN IN ENGLAND . . .

6 9

"I'd totally forgotten that we'd bought"

7 1

"Heaven is where Pushkin reads Tolstoy"

7 2

"What century is it today"

7 3

"My father and my mother, and all my father's"

7 5

"Like a Roman, in general agreement with life"

7 6

Notes on the Poems

7 7

Acknowledgments

8 5

Translators' Acknowledgments

8 7

One of Aleksandr Kushner's poems from the late 1970s begins: "We don't get to choose our century." Kushner does not seem the kind of poet people would quote without knowing, but this line has become a byword in Russia, occurring in everyday speech as if it had been there all along. While it is often cited proverbially, it is also consciously quoted, and sometimes in surprising places, such as in ads and on television. The poem goes on to admonish:

> Nothing on this earth is cruder
> than to beg for time or blame
> the hour . . .
> Though all ages are the iron age,
> lovely gardens steam and varnished
> cloudlets sparkle . . .
>   I embrace
> my age and my fated ending.

Kushner had, by this time, well established the deep grain of stoicism that still informs his work today.

As different as their twentieth centuries were, Kushner's stance dovetails surprisingly with this 1935 statement of Robert Frost's:

> But speaking of ages, you will often hear it said that the age of the world we live in is particularly bad. I am impatient of such talk. We have no way of knowing that this age is one of the worst in the world's history. Arnold claimed the honor for the age before this. Wordsworth claimed it for the last but one . . . I say they claimed

the honor for their ages. They claimed it rather for themselves. It is immodest of a man to think of himself as going down before the worst forces ever mobilized by God . . .

One can safely say after from six to thirty thousand years of experience that the evident design is a situation here in which it will always be about equally hard to save your soul . . . or if you dislike hearing your soul mentioned in open meeting, say your decency, your integrity.

Frost, we believe, would find no fault with Kushner's stance toward his age, or the humility of his bearing toward his times, his art, and his public.

America's image of a Russian poet was shaped by the dramatic biographies of Alexander Pushkin, Mikhail Lermontov, Vladimir Mayakovsky, Osip Mandelstam, Marina Tsvetaeva, Anna Akhmatova, and still others. In a poem that begins "I am mistaken to say that poems take / precedence over biography," Kushner wittily gives Orpheus as his example:

> Fate dealt with him sternly, and his transgression
> Is more precious than if two or three lines
> Of his could be got up for show
> By mama's boy or daddy's little girl.
>
> Not one came down to us—they didn't have to! . . .
> So then, to stick in our minds, in our hearts,
> On leaving hell, be sure to look back. Fall,
> Having dropped your dueling pistol into the snow.
> Or shoot yourself, leaving the chorus to carry on.

More recently, Joseph Brodsky's long residence in the United States gave a new twist to the typology. During Brodsky's trial for "social parasitism" in 1964, Anna Akhmatova ruefully joked, "What a biography they are creating for our red head! You'd think he hired them." And Brodsky's persecution, internal exile, and eventual exile, charged by his own large personality, did indeed become the stuff of legend.

Kushner is well aware of his oblique relationship to this tradition:

> There are poets with a biography, constructing their life in accordance with Romantic conceptions of the poet and his fate, and poets without a biography, relying only on their poems and who make do in them without a lyrical hero. Evidently, I belong to this second category.

And yet, first in his native city, later in the Soviet diaspora, and eventually across the country, Kushner became a popular poet in his own right. Aleksei Tatarinov wrote in a Paris emigré paper in 1985 that "the silent majority of readers knows the worth of his oeuvre. While practically the entire poetry section of the Leningrad division of the Writers Union gathers dust on the shelves of Dom Knigi (The House of Books) on Nevsky Prospect, Kushner sells out in a matter of hours."

What accounts for the popularity of such a modest and quiet voice—without biographical spectacle or flashy linguistic surface? Clearly the first answer is the sheer lyric grace of the poetry. But there are other reasons more particular to time and place.

In a society centered on social ritual and public involvement, Kushner celebrated the resources of private life that were the refuge of the average Russian citizen. Solomon Volkov describes well the other side of those transactions at Dom Knigi: "Kushner was loved in Leningrad for the tenderness of his creations, their refinement, and the dignity with which he defended the right to an independent inner life where pompous state propaganda could not intrude." During his Soviet decades, the intelligentsia—broadly defined—saw themselves in Kushner's plight and admired the energy and integrity of his response.

> We used to write happy verses
> When every last thing stood in our way . . .
>
> In the face of such pressure life still
> Captivated . . .
>
> Love of mine, I will not give you up,
> You, my days, I will not damn to hell . . .
> No one, no one prevented us from reading
> In the evening. I will not divide
> My only life, not in two, or in three.

Kushner had developed a style that was uncannily well poised to span the gulf between Russian cultural tradition and current realities. Utterly natural and contemporary in speech, it is equally traditional and lyrical in form (another way Kushner is like Frost and, still more, like Philip Larkin, an affinity Kushner himself has noted). For native readers of Russian literature, this is further bolstered by a dense web of sonic and substantive allusions to a wide array of earlier Russian writers. Dmitri Bobyshev once remarked that Kushner "is an encyclopedia of Russian poetry." And one reviewer described Kushner's work as "deeply cultured yet down-to-earth."

This pervasive stylistic tension between now and then, like an old-fashioned radio tower flashing its red light all night long, kept pointing out over and over that what was abandoned was not *all* lost, and what had been banished from public life need not be lost to private existence.

While he may be a poet "without a biography," Kushner's life and work very much reflect the major events people lived through in Leningrad/St. Petersburg in the Soviet and post-Soviet periods. Born in 1936, just before the height of Stalin's purges, he lived through the siege of the city in World War II, the "barracks-like" schools, the anti-Semitic campaigns, the poverty and fear of Stalin's postwar regime, the alternations of thaw and repression in the 1960s, the "gray terror" (Olga Sedakova's phrase) of the 1970s, the opening up of late Soviet culture, and the collapse of the Soviet Union—as well as the hopes and disappointments of the last twenty years.

He came of age as a poet in the late 1950s and '60s, a "generational layer in Leningrad" (per Andrei Bitov) that included Bitov, Brodsky, Sergei Dovlatov, Evgenii Rein, and others determined to revive the craftsmanship and sophistication of earlier twentieth-century Russian literature. Naming the writers most admired by his "thaw generation," Kushner grows emphatic: "We did not just *read* the poetry, the prose of [these writers], we lived it." They cherished even more their actual contacts with such survivors as Anna Akhmatova and the critic Lydia Ginzburg, both of whom played significant roles in Kushner's career.

The first of Kushner's eighteen individual books of verse was published in 1962. In the 1960s and '70s, his work was published in Leningrad (i.e., for just the Leningrad market) in modest editions, with a volume appearing every four or five years. Along with Bitov, he was invited to join the Soviet Writers Union in 1965, but his was never one of the strident voices of the sixties. While many of his contemporaries left Leningrad for a life in emigration or the larger stage of Moscow, Kushner's primary loyalty was not to the country at large but to the city of his birth, whatever its name. He has often spoken of his poetry as a conversation with his readers, and the desire to maintain that dialogue has dictated much in the way he has conducted his life and his relationship to the state.

With the advent of the Gorbachev era in the mid-eighties, Kushner's opportunities broadened: a first collected edition of his verse appeared with a print run of a hundred thousand copies, his poems started appearing in major Moscow journals, and he was allowed abroad for the first time to give readings in the United States, where he reunited with Brodsky. While world travel, translations of his work, a teaching stint at Harvard, and honors at home and abroad followed, Kushner is still first and foremost St. Petersburg's resident poet.

This résumé may not be the stuff of legend, but Kushner's consummate modesty and deep stoicism tend to mask how much of "a biography" he *has* had. Readers often marveled at what he was able to publish during the Soviet period, when he worked under constant scrutiny and considerable pressure. When Brodsky praised his clarity of language, lucidity of vision, and sobriety of conscience, he was referring not *only* to what was on the page, but where, when, and in spite of what it had been created. Sobriety of conscience is an apt term. It captures both Kushner's public temper and manner in Soviet times, and his fine balancing of the reality principle with the morality principle throughout.

Kushner's run-ins with Soviet authorities almost always had an anti-Semitic cast, even as late as the *glasnost'* era. Throughout his career Kushner has insisted that he is Russian *and* Jewish and, normally, in that order. He remembers the day he first looked on himself as a Jew. During the siege of Leningrad, he and his mother were evacuated to the city of Syzran on the Volga. His kindergarten teacher began a lesson in "international education."

> She pointed to various kids. "Here's Rustam—he's a Tartar. Here's Alik Kushner—he's a Jew." The kids started to cry out in a friendly way: "He's not a Jew, he's a Leningrader!" At home I asked my mother, "Who are the Jews and why am I one?" I no longer remember how she explained this oddity to me. No, all my life I've lived with the consciousness of a Russian person, but every time I've run up against anti-Semitism, I became a Jew.

Like many of his generation Kushner had no access to religious education or practice. Jewishness tended to come in the form of present danger or tragic memory. His maternal grandmother and several other relatives were killed during the Holocaust. "If I had been born in Germany . . . ," written in the early 1990s, articulates the sentiments of many Russian-Jewish survivors of the war years who chose to stay in the Soviet Union after it became possible to leave:

> If I had been born in Germany in the same year,
> If I'd been born in any European country:
> In France, Austria, Poland—I'd have been lost long ago,

Swallowed into a hell of gas, burnt up by fire like a dry twig.
But I was in luck: I was born in Russia, and, outrageous a spot
As it was—has it known one sweet day?—
Brazen, despotic, beggarly, harrowing,
Hellish—still it gave me a chance to survive.

But I am embarrassed by such arithmetic, to be the remainder
Which only stands out against a backdrop of countless horrors . . .

Still, in the same 2012 interview in which he remembered "becoming" Jewish, he also insists: "In spite of my Jewish roots, I don't believe in the voice of the blood—my whole life is tied to a Russian milieu, to its culture, its poetry."

Note the prominent place of poetry in Kushner's account of his tie to Russia. Adam Zagajewski has spoken of literature as the Great Conversation, a phrase that is very much in the spirit of Kushner's poetic practice. Kushner's bond to Russia expresses itself in the poetry as a rich and resonant conversation with his forebears. While the Great Conversation is universal, the Russian case is special enough for some singling out. Modern Russian literature has always been a small, tight-knit community. Russian writers could, as readers, come close to covering the entire field. (To get a better feel for this, recall the assurance with which English writers of the eighteenth and early nineteenth centuries expected readers to catch their allusions to a common cultural stock.) The memorability and memorizability of poetry intensify this phenomenon still further.

Aleksandr Kushner may be an "encyclopedia of Russian poetry," but he is also its heir. In a realm where this kind of conversation among poets is the norm, he is an acknowledged master. He seems at times like some magus-spider who, scarcely touching a nearby strand, sets off all kinds of answering resonance at the other end of the web. But amid all this intertextual play, Kushner's voice remains unmistakable, and his style distinctive. He plays Russian poetry like an instrument until we hear not just the instrument but the player himself.

Such echoes and ghosts are, alas, untranslatable in their immediacy, at least below the semantic level, at the sonic and phenomenal levels. The notes on the poems will give readers a start on the semantic side of all this dialogue with other writers, but when it comes to the musical quality or feeling tone of an allusion there is little notes can do. And, of course, such elusive properties run through the poems more generally too. It may not be possible to tease out all of the forces that conspire to sustain the sheer lyric grace of Kushner's signature poems and passages, but clearly crucial, along with the dialogic quality we've been discussing, are his natural yet precise tone of voice and rhetorical postures, and the musicality of his Russian, in form, texture, assonance, movement.

Translators simply have to admit that most of the music of most all lyric poetry, and most of its phenomenal presence, stay at home, in the native tongue. But "music of language" is a metaphor. If a language *really* made what we usually mean by music, that music would be intelligible to nonspeakers too. The "music" of language turns out to be deeply dependent on its meaning. As translators we can only hope that, if we faithfully render sense, speech act, image, and tone, and their crucial moments of interplay, not *all* of the "music" will be lost, and some of the world of the poem will survive as not just verbal or visual knowledge but presences in the imagination.

In our eagerness to provide context for the poems, we may have left the impression that Kushner's themes are mainly Russian and Soviet or post-Soviet ones. But another reason for Kushner's popular success was that most of his poems dealt with timeless and everyday matters—and this is still true today. These kinds of poems once offered relief from the crush of history and an affirmation that one's life was already valuable as it stood. Now they can just stand on their own as lyric poems, as so many others have had to do when history disposed of their contexts. And many will stand. For they are beautifully made, and their bearing is universal. But even when Kushner's themes *are* more specific to Soviet and post-Soviet life, they are still not peculiarly Russian, nor are they safely stowed in the past. To borrow Vaclav Havel's phrase, "living in truth" is a universal problem and aspiration, not just a strategy for negotiating a particular moment in the history of oppression. The poems of Aleksandr Kushner represent a lifetime of living in truth and offer much schooling in how it is done.

1988-1996

Аполлон в траве

В траве лежи. Чем гуще травы,
Тем незаметней белый торс,
Тем дальнобойный взгляд держави
Беспомощней; тем меньше слава,
Чем больше бабочек и ос.

Тем слово жарче и чудесней,
Чем тише произнесено.
Чем меньше стать мешает песней,
Тем ближе к музыке оно;
Тем горячей, чем бесполезней.

APOLLO IN THE GRASS

Fine, then, lie in the grass. The thicker it grows
The less conspicuous is the white torso,
That much more futile the long trajectory
Of power's glare; the less glory
The more butterflies here, and wasps.

The more softly the word is pronounced
The more ardent, the more miraculous.
The less it dreams of becoming a song
That much nearer it draws to music,
The more burning, more useless.

The less show it makes of its gloom
The more blameless, the sadder,
Not calling for any loud phrases
About that press, that anvil,
Where, so many times, it was smothered.

Love is tragic, life frightening.
The brighter the white against the green . . .
I don't know what I am guilty of.
The more hopeless the times
The stronger my friendship with Apollo.

The less hope of success
The more room for the soul.
Pierce me, arm me,
With the burning joy of a bee.
Like some great hailstone in the grass—fine, then, lie there.

These days, it would be boring, to be in London, to be in Paris.
Ah, dial up *anyone*, my friend, and the line is busy,
All who lived to see this are phoning one another.
God grant their wish, God grant them strength—and me too, now
    past fifty.

Once again Russia is troubled by a time of great changes.
And I peck at the unforeseen fodder and go looking for groats
From History's hand, so tight with any kindness, slow to nod its
    assent.
"There, not so headlong! Heaven help you!"—but the voice is sullen
    and stern.

I am no dove, no sparrow—And don't you forget
What kind of times I came up in, what darkness I witnessed.
Your time is unmeasured, your law is pegged to the ages,
Out of scale to our lifetimes—and the stern tone is in vain!

Though never the keenest up at the blackboard,
Here's what I know, and could demonstrate from anguish:
You spill, you scatter, grabbing the millet by handfuls, the hemp,
But I love this life despite it all and I do not love you.

Thus a sick man, as he recovers, looks out a window
Where a poplar stands in raw foliage, like a dark stain,
A bundle of hard sinews and outstaring veins.
And yet I feel sorry for those who did not live to see these times.

Nothing brings death closer for us
    Than a desire come to fulfillment.
This is why Venice inspires
Not joy alone but also shudders,
Not just happiness but misgiving.
    Right before us
Uncovered embraces: yearning, and delectation—
And that moist ray of light . . . Danae, put on your dress,

Suck in your stomach, lock your hot bracelets
Back in the box . . . Here they become
    Frightening portents
Of impending doom: happiness comes,
The choice assignment, a trip abroad,
    Keats died in Rome,
And Baratynsky was beguiled by the light blue
Of the waves, the brown skin of the muse.

How they gratify and wear us out—all these changes
    Happening today!
Behind the hangings, hid in the depths,
History stands, like the procuress
In this painting, with her treacherous smile . . .
    Do we recall here the poet—
It was all there before him: he was happy in his mistake—
Or do we believe this sunlight, this bracelet?

What is music?—I do not know.
Could someone please explain it to me?
I enter the white hall, find a place on one side.
Life and death, and a plaint, and shame.

These sounds, how they sing, how they caress!
Many-stringed paradisal sin.
At once I'm seized, put under arrest, and carted off
Right here in front of everyone.

Not me—him! But he buried his face
In his hands and escaped, while I was lost.
For the auditory canal runs straight down
Into the heart, into that dusky flame.

So this is where real embarrassment lies—in hearing!
Life exposed to all its depth.
A moment ago I could look on life dryly.
Now *that* life is brushed off like a tear from a lash.

In this sense we are all unisexual. All of us
Peek through the same paradisal foliage.
You become strange to me, trousers and hemlines.
It is an androgyne who attends on the divine.

And love is totally different then,
Without insults and anguish.
The sound dies away. Expulsion from paradise.
The light is put out—Farewell!—the piano is closed.

I know you, know you, have you down pat, I live in your heart,
Live in your thoughts, like the powder-broom down in the culvert.
Why you don't sleep, why you smile in the dark I know.
Like a mouse behind the paneling, I quiet down in your mind.

I live in your heart, know you, know you, have you down pat,
For seven years—waking and sleeping—I have deputized clouds,
The clouds, the draft that bursts in on us through the open pane,
And that low osier-bed, which grows along the sodden banks.

I know you, know you, why you don't sleep—for you are
Not done yet gathering up the day's spoils
In your mind, entering your hard-won proceeds,
And now it must all be looked over once more, and sorted out.

You must take down a volume of poems—not a large one—
And run through it not just with your eyes but your soul,
And once more, in your mind, twirl through a phone conversation,
I know you, know you, why you're not sleeping even now.

You are not sleeping because water runs through your fingers
And you cannot get it all down, nowhere—not in notebook or journal—
It flows through, pours through, and everything is so suffused
With love and one starry ray that regret is just out of the question.

Give, oh give me the purple slippers with an upgathered toe
And an outfit embroidered in gold, with diamonds and amethysts;
How long can one go around in a sports coat, live on the dull
   brushwork
Of ordinary paintings and their wishy-washy hues?

How long can one read the papers, take one's tea, weary of pretense?
The Mycenean kings are brothers to me: some overthrown, some
   strangled.
One saved by a hasty retreat, one by his impersonation of the garden
   drudge.
After, trembling in the tilted cart—sailed away aboard a ship, sped
   off in a rented car.

Oh how interesting, how interesting to live,
To participate in the world's spectacle,
To be tossed down a sheer drop,
To be found in reeds and unwrapped by a nymph or a stork.

A friend betrays me, I am whispered about behind walls.
I have outlived five rulers, number six I like.
These days, when people speak of the "current mentality,"
I commend to their attention titmice somersaulting in the snow.

Ring, telephone, sing, gruff-throated Chorus, pass them along
Under your cloak, ancient maidservant, those little notes.

For what's the cheapest thing in the world? Tears.
They're not worth a thing. He said to her, "Don't cry, faithful

Greek." What *is* it about myrtle on a hero's sword?
Or, as we would put it these days, on the butt of his machine gun.
In this world only verses are glad to stand, mountainlike,
For the offended, so the line gets a bit humpbacked.

You will fall asleep with a lip bitten raw
Among major drunkards and minor thieves.
But there is one who'll cry at night over you—
Ovid, the world's first social parasite.

The vineyards of his native Italy kept
Appearing, far off, in dreams. And you,
On the train, what do you dream of?
Leningrad's inexpressible winter?

When snow sweeps in from the embankment,
And all but buries Liteiny, a man
Rises up, back to the wind,
In front of a small grocery store.

This is when the new verse line appears,
And it has no equal in power;
And now no defenders are left
To stand up for such precision.

Such a searing anguish
It is granted by right
A hard bunk in the convict-car
Burning up track to outrace fame.

You, soul, *entelecheia*, as you were called
Not by Plato, but that more hard-headed student of his,
You are worn out with sheer wasted ink,
So many lines of derivative language:
It is as though an innocent child were sent
To dwell in a hovel of thieves: we must take hold
Of his sleeve and not let go for anything,
However dismal the times and, unswayed by three-kopek sorrow,
Listen close for a few common roots that are
Surely a blessing, even if still undeciphered.
Just reach out your hand in the dark—there is
A star in the clouds and a breathing among the leaves.

This young Rembrandt, with his feline whiskers,
Thinks highly of himself, and of life as well.
Where's the harm in that—judge for yourself:
Wasn't there one who was worse yet at that age?

Is the sun going to rise into the sky tomorrow?
Is life going to end with us?—judge for yourself.
It's a shame, how suspicion grows with the years,
Those eyes burning with trust are so beautiful!

That shade of brown, more precisely, tobacco—
It's still hard to make out here who is cat and who mouse.
Not had enough yet, of the gloom, the circumspection?
Play with me, Fate, he begged, a little longer.

So, this buried malevolence keeps surfacing of its own will,
Until you're prepared to give way, to part with life and drag it
Down with you fast as you can into the grave—
But I am ashamed in front of the painter.

No one will ever wear a hat as he does, that's for sure.
A velvet one, with a soft, fluted brim.
And how can one upbraid him, especially from where we stand,
Knowing how, later, the darkness will thicken?—judge for yourself.

There where it's Spring, Spring, always Spring,
Where tender foliage eases the slope, and there
Are no black slanders, what a prize will Apollo
Confer on me!—that god dreamed up for poets.

While, here, the trunk of the poplar, overgrown tip-to-toe
With thick leaves, wreathes itself until it is lion-maned.
For bringing motifs like no others into this world
And a foreshortening all my own.

For, in an age when ideas went prowling the land
Like predators prowling the dark,
Praising the white cloth on the table
With its design as subtle as watermarks.

A poet is to critics as a boy is to flogging.
But I did not dance to that pipe.
For being deeply ashamed of these lines,
And renouncing them and making mock.

For gathering a certain music, like water into a sieve,
For those who lived the same way, on the margins,
For pliancy and the like, and for *Not on your life*,
And for *je vous aime, ich liebe.*

Dear Aleksandr, here where I write from, we have neither
The sirens (ah! the sirens with their mad voices!)
    Nor the Cyclops—sitting
In their offices with their eyes, everything shipshape,
Over each a portrait on duty—Tell them all I say Hi.

We have no outlaws, no nymphs; however sad to say,
Apartments and grottoes, that's all there is.
    As for rhymes,
As you can see, I've gotten the hang of that child's play
In a foreign tongue, recalling still the tides' ebb and flow.

    A wave rustles
Bringing a wide-bellied bottle to my feet, a note
    From my beloved country . . .
Here where I write from, the sea sticks to the setting sun's disk
And the disk won't go down: dreams that don't "set" become torments.

    Dear Aleksandr,
Next I'll explain why I chose you. True, much closer to me
Is unruly Archilochus, or old seven-string Terpander,
But a palm tree dreams of a pine, in its own snow-lit reddish beauty,
    Not some gorse or oleander.

And, besides, the choice
Fell on unsociable you because, being the stay-at-home,
You skirted the islands, did *not*, by a mere eyelash, drop into the dark
Beyond Lethe, you said all you cared to, didn't deceive,
    And remained

In anonymity's gracious shade. But when you die all you have said
Will be sorted out, much as an emerald or diamond's flame
    Is drawn up to the eye.
How many grotesques you had to twist onto your finger! Don't fear
    their articles,
Their fantasies—It's you who are deluded, literary gang!

You who are deluded, like that grazing herd of suitors.—
    The traitor's lotos
Remains untasted, and you have still your homeland, your sorrows,
And your sins. A man dies, but verses survive.
Hail to the gentle mind and straightforward, masculine meekness.

Whether you, like me, were aided by God or by the swarthy gods,
Emerging as from a niche or the airy pit of a dream,
    The chill embraced you,
Wafting love across to a country strewn with snow . . .
I embrace you. Odysseus. (No need to reply.)

The only thing better than Delft in this world is this Delft on canvas.
I was looking close at the yellow, dark blue, rose-colored wall.
Why oh why have I been given so lavish a present?

How he loved the textures of things, my favorite novelist!
He offered death to his hero, like joy, like a fresh page.
This moisture, dampness, the gloss on the lilies' batiste.

The lilies swim prettily on their small green plates.
They bloom, they prosper in the shade of sleepy canals.
To think now on things, on people lost—Heaven forbid!—

It is wrong-headed, offensive—as it would be in paradise.
I have wondrously distanced my life from myself.
Soviet power, the seething Congress, raging discord back home . . .

To ride a bike, sit in a café, peruse in a paper
What they have to say about Moscow?
Why in the world is one life allotted, not two?

The whole surface of this small city is crazed by a watery spiderweb.
It's much too easy, is it not, to die here in front of the painting
A quick, sparrow-like death—one's cup of pride will not allow it.

I'll tell you what I finally understood, what I arrived at. The meaning's
Right there on the palm of your hand, evident, palpable: God
    conceived,
And I played it out, in this world of sorrows, this sea of troubles.

A wee bit of a bird putters around at my feet.
Now my words chime with the novelist's, and the painter's my kin.
Life is a searing habit, a solid gold snare.

It is frightening to live and, by the same token,
Not to live is *not* frightening. A happy dream—
Endless, even and deep, with us
Left out. To gain detachment
From attached rooms, alcoves,
Streets, friendships, conversing, doors . . .
I recall hearing in boyhood, "Time to get up!
You'll sleep through it all!"

To sleep through it all! There is no more
Carefree condition. Already I've slept through
Troy, Diaghilev's ballet,
Olympia in her nightie,
Herod's entourage leaving the palace,
Pushkin dashing out from the porch . . .
Why sigh, mourn, turn away from
The end, why cover your face?

I am mistaken to say that poems take
Precedence over biography, that what remains
Is the word and not the poet's image.
The example of Orpheus shakes my conviction.
Fate dealt with him sternly, and his transgression
Is more precious than if two or three lines
Of his could be got up for show
By mama's boy or daddy's little girl.

Not one came down to us—they didn't have to! Stalactites
Hang there like tears, anguish, the cold . . .
So then, to stick in our minds, in our hearts,
On leaving hell, be sure to look back. Fall,
Having dropped your dueling pistol into the snow.
Or shoot yourself, leaving the chorus to carry on.
But poems . . . that's a separate conversation,
A professional one, and disinterested.

Only once did our cold hands entwine . . .

—IN. ANNENSKY

I think I know where the anguished note comes from—
There is really nothing quite like it,
You don't hear it in Tyutchev or Fet—
Oh! The almost criminal pain, and the worry!
And that's what gave us such a poet!
Not in vain did he translate Euripides.
A moist, clandestine sun, as we have in March.
Having locked it all in, you've brooded hard, and kept up
Appearances—he must leave not a clue, and give it up!
The shrinking snow and the blank pain.
It's a masculine version of Phaedra.
And in a frock coat it's even worse,
And the silk tie foils consolation,
And the bland snow, and the Spring light,
And the stables squatting in steam, and the starling houses—
Growing more and more hopeless and more fraught with farewells.

THE WATERFALL

To renew the wish to live, I remember a waterfall.
It clutches at stones, hangs like a wild grapevine
In a blind homeland of stone letters, stone books—
Here's the one who takes life in totally, perishing every instant.

All Shakespeare's eloquence is second-hand, a little brother.
Here's the one who's glad to take his life—for the very love of it!
Here's where each year counts for three, and lips are set free;
Every last seat in the stony amphitheater is taken.

Let chapel mount on chapel there, one on the other,
And blunt-topped mountains lie, pillow on pillow.
Don't drag me to the car—faithful if sullen man that I am . . . Why
Even the wind at the peak is a sluggard beside it!

After such interlacing of swarthy arms and sloping shoulders,
No mere human's seething rage still feels hotheaded to me.
It is *alive*, and you . . . are living, getting along, dying
A little, chewing it all over: life, wishes, clouds . . .

We used to write happy verses
When every last thing stood in our way.
The threads of a fringe would be disturbed, and a peek
Would be periscoped to the tablecloth's embroidered flowers—
Long live that very detail, the fools had it under surveillance!
And, ray of sun, then too, you would come to rest
On my fingertips. Come, keep me company—but oh!
You were always like that—you'd slip off and be gone.

In the face of such pressure life still
Captivated. Now, with every last thing permitted,
We'll just have to see what the daredevils will
Come up with next, what sort of films we're going to get . . .
I think back to *There Once Lived a Song Thrush*,
That nocturnal music running all through it,
House in Tbilisi, long Georgian toast,
A sleeper's dream-struggle with the moon.

Love of mine, I will not give you up,
You, my days, I will not damn to hell . . .
No one, no one prevented us from reading
In the evening. I will not divide
My only life, not in two, or in three.
A wondrous meaning would flare up, then die down.
Neither, you could be sure, did the garden rustle for nothing—
And we were understood from half a word!

TROY

TO TOMAS VENCLOVA

Can you believe it (said my friend) all of Troy
Out of a space not much bigger than this
Little square, this small playground for tots,
So that, when the enraged Achilles lapped it three times,
He didn't lose all that much breath
Catching up with the offender . . . Then I imagined this
Little Troy as it got covered in dust, overgrown
With vegetation, and I have to admit, I grew quiet.

Can you believe it, all of Troy
Begins with this small courtyard, this sandlot . . .
I don't know what a historian would say
But I'm quite pleased to wonder aloud
If greatness is not sooner scaled to the heart
Than to anything very enormous.
So it was with Hector, Odysseus,
Little doubt, it's the same way today.

In despair or in trouble, trouble,
Whoever you may be, when you go down in sorrow,
Know this: I've been there before you on this murky star,
I've gone cold, I've wept in the hallway.

So as not to be noticed, I lowered my eyes. I admit to you
These tears of my own, unfortunate friend,
Whoever you may be, just so you'll know: the heavens
Will not be struck by that thick, silent cry,

And they will not reply. Don't you see the ancient track?
You are not the first to thread the shadows along the precipice.
The path is laid. There then, isn't that better?
Touchy one, I'm playing with you.

You'd like me to spell out my misfortunes? They will not
Pass my lips; the thick-skinned bush is still smoldering.
Like that moment in Pushkin: "it's all coming down on my head . . ."
What is this "all"? Don't ask: all of us have the same all.

Ah, you, whoever you may be, aren't you
Already less wretched, less lonely?
Pace the room back and forth, or lie down on the sofa awhile,
And here's life, up and about again, tender, blue-eyed.

1997 – 2004

X   X   X
"... тише воды, ниже травы..."
А. Блок

Когда б я родился в Германии в том же году,
Когда я родился, в любой европейской стране:
Во Франции, в Австрии, в Польше, – давно бы в аду
Я газовом сгинул, сгорел бы, как щепка в огне,
Но мне повезло – я родился в России, такой,
Сякой, возмутительной, сладко не живется ни дня,
Бесстыдной, бесправной, замученной, полунагой,
Кромешной – и выжить был всё-таки шанс у меня.

И я арифметики этой стесняюсь чуть-чуть,
Как выгоды всякой на фоне бесчисленных бед.
Плачь, сердце! Счастливый такой не вернуть
С гербом и печатью районного загса билет
на вход в этот ужас? Но сказано: ниже травы
И тише воды. Средь безумного вихря планет!
И смотрит бесслёзно, ответа не зная, увы,
Не самый любимый, но самый бесстрашный поэт.

. . . lower than grass, quieter than water . . .

—ALEKSANDR BLOK

If I had been born in Germany in the same year,
If I'd been born in any European country:
In France, Austria, Poland—I'd have been lost long ago,
Swallowed into a hell of gas, burnt up by fire like a dry twig.
But I was in luck: I was born in Russia, and, outrageous a spot
As it was—has it known one sweet day?—
Brazen, despotic, beggarly, harrowing,
Hellish—still it gave me a chance to survive.

But I am embarrassed by such arithmetic, to be the remainder
Which only stands out against a backdrop of countless horrors.
Cry, Heart! Granted this boon, why should he *not* return his ticket
For admission into the horror, with its stamp and seal from the Registry?
But, as the saying goes: lower than grass
And quieter than water. Amid the mad whirlwind of the planets!—
He looks on, without a tear, though, alas, not knowing the answer,
Not my best-loved, but our most fearless poet.

Do not inquire of God: He is not in this world.
The heavenly kingdom is . . . heavenly, its light unearthly.
The earth receives just a few glimmers.
So most of the world lies in evil.

Useless, then, to sprinkle holy water
Over the raised barrels of the youthful
Guard-unit, open-mouthed, like birds.
Grave doubts concerning the holy water, grave doubts

Concerning right conduct, and left conduct as well.
The only deeds still standing are those that aimed
Beyond Earth's horizons, and these are very few.
At times, in the binoculars, one makes out

A distant headland, licked by sun, swaddled in foam.
All the rest is delusion or falsehood.
And you live in the dusk, and I in total darkness.
And only the ray means anything, gliding along my sleeve.

Poems are anachronisms. And soon they'll disappear.
It seems laughable to insist still on that bird-like
Twittering to which Archilochus woke us so early,
And that clings still, like some thistle-creature.

Farewell, speaking in measure. Prose is here to relieve you.
So what if the newcomer has no Muse? Your lyric ardor
Stands out like a pose against this backdrop
Of relentless newspapers and magazines.

I was drinking with a prose writer. All the while
He was telling me stories. As ever, a story bears the impress
Of a particular worldview, but a verse line lives
Without purpose, flies like the swallow, freely, at will.

And it is clearly impossible to imagine iambs
In the third millennium. What would it do with them?
That's how it goes. How could I mourn so small a loss?
No, don't complain, mourn and burn, right down into the dark.

On seeing that cottage where you and I lived
Seven years back, I wanted to stop, but got cold feet.
I was younger there, and you were different:
More fearless with evil, and life was working less hard,
Not roughly, as now, but more politely, in moderation,
To tighten its knot about you. And those
With whom the transparent-winged sea winds
Promised us a meeting somehow—they were still living.

On seeing that cottage under the cedars, in the shade
Of their over-grown, bear-brown branches,
I thought that we or, to speak more honestly, they
Would startle the me of today—such apparitions
Off time's reel are acceptable in film, with its spurts
And ruptures, but, in person, they would be ghastly:
Banter would flag, voices fall silent,
The pace would slow—the joke fall flat.

Live there without us then, kiss in the dark
And, at midday, swim out fearlessly beyond the buoys . . .
On seeing that cottage I understood why
Ghosts can cause terror. Don't feed those
Illusions—or else do: something delectable,
Something sweet. Perhaps, then, as once on Ithaca,
On seeing that cottage, I will overcome the day's anguish
And will smile in the dark.

If the city of Peter had been established on the Black Sea,
If our Tsar had pushed, tear-faced, all the way down to the Bosphorus,
We would not have these faces in which anguish and cold agree,
But would enjoy Fortune's favor and live in her good graces.

We would find in our canals certain nereids splashing about,
Nothing at all like this creature made of snow and bruises;
Common sense would be one of our heroes, one of our gods,
And such waking dreams would not haunt us, nor insult abuse us.

If the city of Peter had marched, vineyard-like, down a mountain
To terraced waves, in a long file of trees,
No idol would have soared, then, across the abyss, no Bronze
    Horseman
Hurtled off to come down on corpses—or living bodies.

No need for the axe tucked under one arm, nor the overcoat;
Side by side through the ages with Venice!
And, under our eyelids, you would find pastel blue dreams afloat:
The Pillars of Hercules, and the wings of Icarus.

THE SUGARBOWL

IN MEMORY OF L. IA. GINZBURG

How does it live without you, your belonging, does it pine?
Not in the least! I saw that, with others, in a different time,
Like Pushkin's Olga, it does not remain
True to the dead, and has forgotten its old home.

Otherwise, it would be unbearable.
With its four curving feet, and its silvery belly—
But no! Here too it is valued, does not want
For anything, does not look back for anyone,

Adorns the table and, if the conversations are not quite
What they were there—a bit simpler, a little less rich—
All the same, the monograms and flourishes shine,
And, soldered there to one side, what looks like a little angel.

Even so, I took it into my hands for a moment,
Heavy as a dream, put it down, and averted my eyes.
And what was I expecting? That it show distress?
Burst into tears? Strew the granules onto the table?

LETTERS

As you can see, in Latin script
The hills of Rome are depicted,
Lamb's curls of Mediterranean whitecaps,
A tangle of scales and ringlets—the herd
Will have already started to climb while
The shepherd sucks wine from a handflask.

But then, the Georgian alphabet was shattered
Into small shards by a sword,
Or flung itself from a steep
Shelf. The morning mist gives a
Slight shiver—Titsian, Paolo, and Ilya
Gather up each little round chip.

But in the Russian *zhe* and *sha*
The soul lives as a soul should—
A blizzard, roaring and foaming, sweeps through,
And a spry coachman, red-cheeked, daring and tipsy,
With a hand at each hip of his caftan,
Steers the little horse through.

And here is High German letterpress
Where the characters' Gothic thickness
Makes it hard to tell one from another,
Huddling there like the rooftops
Of Marburg. Calls in the night, sound of steps.
Careful, don't rouse them! Softer! Softer!

A Jewish letter takes to the air—
Where to?—how should it know where?—
When the words are all written like notes.
So take up the old violin, then,
Press the handkerchief to your chin
And don't wail, play . . . Oh but, there, what's the matter, what is it?

Riding into the city, you see the warehouses,
Rusty iron drums and piles of brick;
You see old viaducts, wild architectural
Oddments, loading docks leading nowhere,
All of which must, no doubt, warm the hearts
Of whiners and misanthropes.

The haters-of-life, starting out from this hard crust,
Run aground on distraction and happenstance.
And, in this twilight zone, I understand them!
Riding into the city, you see candlesticks
Of poplars; over them, a flock of crows,
Under them, a train car—not exactly enticing:

A hideous, useless, rusted-out pullman,
Just the place to bring those to be tortured—
And, showing through the outer wall,
A bloody bruise. You see the viscera of machines,
Pulled-out pieces, while, in the stuffy depot next door,
A diesel sits, snug as in a pencil box.

A kingdom of scrap iron and shattered glass
And—antediluvian marvel!—a steam locomotive;
Transformers stripped of their wires, bobbins
No longer covered by cable, derelict wheels—
As if a gigantic Pliushkin sneaks in and out
Powered by Gogol's nerves and psychosis.

It leaves you vaguely ashamed, like trashy thoughts,
Dirt from the subconscious, the common horrors
Of everyday life, the unwashed sheets
And bad breath. Write it off
To the same scrap heap as the Obvodny Canal,
Or those blind alley apartment blocks.

The Messiah will not be coming for us—don't worry.
Or hope. Emissaries from another planet,
Having flown in and run up against
The likes of this, these utterly material tokens—
Grazed by their mortal sadness,
Will soon stash their heroism and clear out.

Good riddance, then. We don't need them. Give me your hand.
Smile. I'm not griping, am not aggrieved
That I lived, that the Earth revolves in its circuit
Among the stars; I know how to bring myself around.
If you'd like, I'll go over those verses on dirt and torment
And what may, perhaps, lie behind them.

I must think this through to conclusion.
　　　　The stars glow in the clear sky.
　　　　　　Weak-sighted pollen.
There is still, in this time, good reason
To admire the Creator's artistry.

A star; by the porch, wild roses, growing profuse;
　　　　Holly; the river's brink;
　　　　　　The great windows of a palace;
And the sweet paleness of a beautiful face—
As Fet reminded us skeptics—and egotists.

Whether I believe in God or do not believe in god,
The road to Vyritsa knows how things are,
Night's wave, in Crimea, knows how things are,
Whether I was open or was closed to him.

And it strikes you first glance that, here, I've written his
Name with the capital and, there, with the lower-case letter,
To you, this is important, to Him, it does not matter.
The star that bursts through my window—it knows,

It knows—the opened book, and the little stand with its journals.
Don't grieve, dear friend, don't mourn, little darling.
Something has happened in five thousand years.
The question has withered away and the answer shed all its meaning.

And, in general, such matters are private—*private*, precisely.
And it's not to still water but to water that's flowing
I would liken the soul: the water runs by.
No—it says down in the shadow, but up in the sunlight—yes!

Maybe this life is all one poem,
With flowers on the table, love and loss,
   And out past the border of days, past the edge
Of doom, they'll ask us what we thought of it,
And, no, not rage, not caprice, but inspiration seized hold
Of the author, and you and I simply did not understand.

Beautiful poems need fear no ill fortune,
   Tears do not spoil them,
Madness suits them, and they are slightly bitter,
Like the sweet scent of blown acacias lining the boardwalks
By the seashore. There is no cause to feel pity.
Well then! it crashed, well! withered, well! died, well! it faded.

And when, late at night, we were reciting verses,
Faltering, coming to each other's aid,
Didn't we feel then, precisely,
   That they were stronger than the rain
Making a racket in the back garden, more sullen
Than scraps of cloud with glimmering, dawn-gilded edges?

They must have known all this already—
   Those who died young
Like Keats or Shelley (and unlike us),
So Lermontov, flying by like a star—never to stale
   Or get lost in details—
Having grasped things by their essence, spurned any compromise.

FAREWELL TO THE CENTURY

TO ANDREI AR'EV

Go, get out—this is how we spoke
To the century, like some hanger-on—
You were too gloomy, too exhausting,
To some niche with you, some reference work, some archive!
So it stomped around a bit—and left.

We parted quietly, without a tear.
As if we could care less if we
Never heard of it again—and why?
Last year's fly came back to life and flits around now,
Finding everything quite satisfactory.

The nineteenth was fond
Of its half-sleeping, armchair dreams,
Dreams it would change with its gloves.
The eighteenth was enlightened
Or at least believed in reason—and you?

Look at yourself, what a lowlife you are,
A communist, a total fascist, to put
The best face on it: an avant-gardist.
Could even a mother love such a one?
Last year's brown leaf.

And yet I feel sorry for it somehow, with its rock-steady
Step, with its bright spots and shadows.
For, in fact, didn't I live there, didn't I love there?
And wasn't it born under the sign
Of volcanic theories and forces?

With Pasternak, and Shostakovich,
And the telltale swelling of communal graves.

I looked at the poet and thought: it's a good thing
He's writing verse and not ruling Rome
For, in both, power's the idiom
And, once in his grip, we wouldn't last
A single year—he would shackle us all
In iron stanzas where life's enjambment
Falls on the side of glory and catastrophe.
Hounding tyrants, he was one himself;
And my head would surely have rolled
For its lyrical gift and a love of objects
Irrelevant to his stately successes,
Warmed by a light decidedly softer.

But in verse, this power of his, with its cry of a hawk
And its disdain for the two-footed—jealously fixed
On the stars—would seize my heart in a happy instant,
One unimaginable to Caligulas or Terribles,
And dazzle me, lifting me over the clouds
Into a chase I too know well. Even so,
I would implore him: Please, not so loud, give back
My room, my armchair and armrest!
—And he loved and tyrannized me.
Still, my taste leans more to swallows running the blue
Cloth through their scissors, swiftly shearing
The sky's distant edge. He kissed me: It's your funeral.

Here's what I envy: Prussian blue,
Deep cobalt blue—the sea reaches
In a slender band from behind
The mountains and it streams like smoke;
Having gone back through my life,
I envy red ochre, verdurous earth;
Leave a tube of the color "P. Veronese"
Beside me here on the table,
Arrange the near, out-spilling foreground
So that its leaves brocade the sun,
And the English would understand me,
The Japanese would take me up.

Oh brilliant yellow, give me heart,
Carmine and madder lake, serve me here
In place of the word, which requires translation,
And still winds up in the dark.

The artist is at a loss
To explain: come up and look.
He's used to creeping through ribgrass
As prose stylists do through *Madame Bovary.*
What I envy him are his gestures, his exclamations,
His bellowing, the glister of zinc white,
Not his opinion—some remark
As to the honey tone of the banister.

I too would brighten my palette,
But the old earthly horror restrains me,
The passerby on his artificial limb,
The neighbor's sick child.
I could sit out on the grass
In a sailor-stripe vest and straw hat,
Sipping now and again from my flask,
And disown the murky word.
For I do envy ultramarine, and how
The laundry hangs on the line . . .

I will never ever leave you,
black and white word of mine!

When, in the end, that teacher in Poland,
So as to not abandon the orphans, accompanied them
Down into hell, and the new Herod
Could exult in his villainous feat,
Where was this God that you love?
Or is he, as Berdyaev thought, weaker
Than the weakest of scoundrels, a bit of smoke
Behind the clouds, a mere puff?

Just a shade, then, among the shades,
An eccentric, frankly, a loser; and any
Of those red-haired German machine-gunner lads
Is stronger, and more dependable, than he.
And, as for innocents slaughtered,
Bible stories are teeming with them.
No one, you can be sure, in those days
Gave them a second thought.

But no philosophical teaching
Can damp down my distress,
And such an unearthly coolness
Arouses in me nothing but loathing.
The only permissible God
Goes with the children into the chambers,
Evil hiked high on his shoulder,
Like that old teacher in Poland.

VENICE

You know, the best road in the world
Just may be that slippery one
Which runs from palace to palace,
Its water lapping right under them,
Where wooden pilings stick up on end
And, tied on their tethers in a row,
Catafalque-shaped black flocks
Stand idle so elegantly.

We floated along its golden tresses
Close by cliff-like ruins
Built in the Moorish style
But echoing Alp and Apennine,
And those steps, rising out of their
Coating of velvety green, reminded us both
Of our gloomy genius of Muranovo
And his "sepulchral Aphrodite."

So crumble! drown! fade away! That's the truth
Of the matter. Colder and colder age by age.
This path is only the dearer if the buildings
Repeat the sufferings of the people.
Otherwise, why would the morning glories
And geraniums blaze so
From each niche and portal,
And on the balconies, greeting the dark?

To close, then (I must abbreviate
My delight), floating together down this path
Was like passing along life's edge,
Where it appears not as fire
Flaring out into the darkness, but as water
Riddled with lights—beyond all harm—
As sweet unrest, as lucky calamity.
For everything flows. And, at the same time, burns.

BUSHES

Look at these bushes
Hugging the hillside: this one
Here's my best buddy! And I am
Just as shaggy, as overgrown.

Saving the landscape
From vertigo, asking no one,
It simply appears,
Anchorite, and guardian.

Look in close among the branches:
A flame flares up precisely when
It is least visible to our glances,
At light of noon.

There is something, then, here on
Earth on which heaven will risk
Its trust—and it could even flare up
Right here, on my desk.

The bush remembers, sees all.
And, as in that most ardent
Of books, there is no telling who'll
Step out of it next instant.

A PHOTOGRAPH

I think this is the village of Mezhno,
Or, perhaps, Pribytkovo. The year, thirty-nine.
The grown-ups found it amusing,
The children were made to sit on a little slope.
The photographer told them to smile. A place
In the clouds, it smells of clover and mint.

Of these six old-style children
(Today no one wears such dresses or bows)
One is known to me. Don't be timid,
I want to whisper to him, there are various
Fates and possibilities; the wind over the fields
Is so sweet, and the gods are by no means sticklers.

I cannot believe they are perfidious,
Rather they're clumsy, or just lazy.
There must be butterflies somewhere here
In the meadow, even if not shown in the photo,
So vague, so washed-out. The horizon is like
A strung bow, beyond lies uncertainty, possibly danger.

Of these six there is one I could call by name
In his worn cap and rumpled sailor's jacket.
Why am I sorry not for him but the others?—
He's alive. Them, life has erased, dissolved,
Blotted out. Are *any* left? Photographer,
Clean your lenses better!

The three boys are nondescript. But the girls
Are charming, a smile comes to them more easily.
I am three—and that burning sensation,
Like the sun, has scarcely entered my ken.
Hey, look, steal a peek at the girl!
Until you look, her soul won't stir.

But the boy looks submissively at the lens.
How to find out what's on his mind, if he's okay?—
And the sudden gust of wind—is it
Pleasant for him, or is it cold in the field?
Remember, the negative is not developed yet,
Fates and roles are not yet handed out.

The boy has a Russian appearance. His hair
Is lighter than it will be. The children are mollusk-like,
Unassigned still, hard to place in the schema.
Having no place, they don't need hideouts and shutters.
You will be a Tartar woman, you, a Jew.
It's not true that, having been born in Russia, you're a Russian.

It looks to me like the grass is prickly,
And the hill hunches awkwardly, rigidly.
As usual, happiness comes into its rights
Only post facto, and, so, is too unwieldy, and tedious.
The children barely know each other—the sailor jacket
Cuts into the flesh under his armpit.

At three, a person is held from the darkness
By only three half-swooning years,
Isn't yet really at home on earth,
Is still poised to change places with death.
In a distance somehow bordered by bushes,
The hazy horizon holds nothing.

I wish that of this small handful, these six, someone
Besides me was still alive, that the blockade's snare
Had spared him, the steep paths and hillsides,
And that, preserving this snapshot in a family album
In much the same way, he too was gazing,
Long-sighted, into the past.

I wish that he or she too was looking for
This same region of life, earth, forgotten planet, village,
For this little hill rising like a cottage loaf
In the July heat. Not a snapshot, but a pass
To a lost paradise. No, not paradise,
But certain inklings, or its first outlines.

2005–2010

Вечерней мглою был сведён на нет
И сад и ели контур грандиозный,
И если в окнах церкви брезжил свет,
То свет, скорей всего, религиозный,
Оставшийся или от служб дневных,
Или молитв старушечьих, прилежных.
Есть в сельской церкви то, что городских
Людей влечёт, и самых безнадёжных.

Таких, как я, — сознанью вопреки
И горькой очевидности явлений.
А может быть, присутствие реки
И сумрачность шуршаний, шелестений
Поддерживали этот слабый свет
И сердцу втайне что-то говорили,
Не требуя ответить: да иль нет,
Не заставляя выбрать: или — или.

Evening dark brought down to nothing
Both the small garden and the fir's grandiloquent outline
And if, in the church windows, a light still gleamed,
Most likely, it was a devotional one,
Left either from the day's service
Or the old women's dutiful praying.
There's something about a village church which attracts
City folk, even the most hopeless—

Such as I—in spite of all conscious knowledge
And the bitter evidence of phenomena.
Perhaps, though, the river's presence
And the night's murky rustling and whirring
Were shoring up this weak light
And saying right into the heart something
That called for no answer, no yes-or-no,
Required no choice, no either-or.

Having overcome barriers, rises, and steps,
More and more often at night departed friends
Enter my dreams as spectral shades.
I look at them—and the salons crowd me in,
And the little rooms too—and they beckon me after,
But perhaps something—a pillow, a sheet,
A shred of reason—keeps an eye on me
And will not let me mingle with them.

Just as a viewer passes along a frieze or a fresco
Where priests process like folds in a curtain,
Or warriors, or captive kings, and, look, he is ready
To become one of them, and would this very moment
Were it not for the jacket, the tie, that make him
Bristle and hold back from stepping into
Their flowing formation as they descend
Toward eternity into the darkness in single file.

STATUE

This Roman with his upraised arm,
This marble idol of the park,
How pathetic he is, what an agonizing fate
Befell the poor man, to freeze in the cold.

The wind blows, tearing leaves off the aspens,
Heralding January's torments.
Even at night, when he's quite alone,
He cannot let himself lower his arm.

Everyone admires a statue, its beauty,
Indifference, or repose. They too would
Stand like that at the pomerium
Before the pale, barbaric throng.

The darkness around him eats at his eyes,
Then the pre-dawn hoarfrost gnaws.
And as once his gesture failed to save Rome,
Neither will he be able to defend us.

The garden's freshness was there in the room.
A window was opened wide to the night.
The rain murmured—delightful, cool.
The dark was just slightly bitter, like wine.

One could make out an apple tree
By the angular lines of its branches.
And under it, a wheelbarrow, two shovels,
The circle of soil at its base, moisture, abundance!

I've always thought that I am not worthy
Of this life: but what's our flattery to it?
And breathing the dark, the rich scent in small gulps,
I see that, yes, that *is* how it is.

I hadn't decided about the mosquitoes—
Turn on a light and they swoop in.
Having gathered my robe, I stretched
My hand toward the sash in the dark,

Then changed my mind—better to sit awhile
Without a light, without a book, stay just like this,
Have a smoke to make it easier
To survive this trial by happiness.

Vesuvius preserved these frescoes for us.
If it hadn't erupted neither the female dancers
Nor the duck with the spear of grass in its bill
Nor the gold flowers and fish would have reached us.

I love this villa of mysteries,
The flagellants, the naked Bacchante,
Such a red as I've never seen!
The yellow cloak with its brown lining.

So thank you, slivery ash,
Corner brace, pumice, stone rain,
For preserving all this magnificence!
But don't you pity the perished Pompeians?

Given the choice, which would you choose: the art
Or the lives of these Romans, the men and women?
You'd choose their lives. And so would I. Isn't it sad?
For, after all, life is short, and doesn't shine with anything.

I burned a small hole in my pants—above the knee—
And thought, well, I won't wear these again.
Later I got over it and began wearing them
Anyway, and hardly anyone noticed: Who'd care
Really? Who would study us that closely?
And here's what happened: Venice glittered
Like a moist netting thrown over life.
We chose a table under an awning by the Rialto Bridge
And sat down in the open air and drank wine.
It was as though we were being run through the scenes
Of an old film, or an irresistible dream—
How could one *not* light up a cigarette?
But wafting in from the Canal, a breeze
Arose—on purpose, perhaps—and a speck
Of burning tobacco fell on my trousers
So that I would not forget this moment.

In the first century everything was supposed to end,
And a different everything was supposed to begin.
But it didn't end. Rivers flowed just the same,
And tears flowed from eyes, just the same—like a river.

For some reason the Day of Judgment was postponed,
Ships sailed the seas their same old way,
Changing tack with the shifting wind,
In hot, white foam, like horses in lather.

Man loves what is close by, does not wish evil,
Believes in salvation, and awaits his Messiah
A month, a year, but then grows weary, mutters,
And sinks under grief—like us in Russia.

Or is it that God became so inured to earthly sorrow,
Grew so enamored of the Earth's beauty, that he came
To place it ahead of morality, and is now
Walking behind us on the same path through the forest?

Can you imagine what sort of poet
Dostoevsky would have made? For once
We got lucky. It's scary to think about
All the boundaries swirling off at his advance.

How some gypsy gal would have kissed him
Or, taking aim at his prominent forelock,
Threatened him with a cocked pistol.
Next to him, a pale epigone Blok!

Here it is to a T, that premeditated city,
Steeped in pestilential miasma,
Or cut just like that! as by lightning
Straight through The Haymarket's plaza.

Even a maple leaf, then, could menace,
Raising its hand, popping its veins at passersby.
And just imagine those bony fists of his
Giving anapestic trimeter a try!

How the Jew, German, and Pole
Would be swept to a corner with brooms,
How orthodox infants would carol,
Wafting out unearthly dreams.

And any squabble his conscience gets snared in—
For him, it's all in a day,
But to us, by comparison,
The revolution would seem like child's play.

Do svidaniya, then, my bookcase.
In Russia no more will forests,
Or fields or grasslands still hold a place,
But only this terrifying book of verses.

Shakespeare was mistaken to suppose
Their dreams torment the monsters.
Richard the Third—impressionable,
Visited by guilt—what naïveté!

We, though, know just how well they sleep,
Sending one after the other to be shot.
You are a twig, one more woodchip,
You burn well, the smoke scatters.

Governing life by governing death,
The regime swells and expands.
What it needs its idea for
Is to stir vicious passion.

A LITTLE PICTURE

MADE FROM BLOCKS

A little picture made from blocks, it's almost complete.
See: it's a lion. There's still a gap in the mane,
And some hitch occurred with the tail, but there's time—
Make it right, puzzle over it a little longer, don't rush
To fill in the last blanks. Well, here's the beast;
The game's nearly done. What's the matter?—
Don't get upset that it's a lion. It could have been a hare,
Or an elephant like a gray mountain,

And you got a lion, you did a good job. No one's to blame
That your childhood fell during wartime, that the century's
Burning hot jaws breathed in your face,
That you were handed a tough country,
That dark thoughts came in the night to overpower you,
That this menacing lion never befriended the little billy.
Yet think: the King of the Beasts! There are things
You understood better than those who made a duckling.

I was standing in front of the best equestrian statue
In the world—and it enthralled me.
A condottiere in Venice or Padua,
The Russian tsar where the river laps by—
They can't compare with this Roman emperor.
Why?—don't ask just yet.
Leave me to commune with myself,
To keep faith with my vague instinct.

If you dismiss life's mortal noise and look well
At this other bronze one, then you will see:
It's that the steed steps so slowly,
That the rider knows no despair.
It's because haughtiness is simply boring,
And cruelty is not dear to my heart,
While what *is* dear is this deep pensiveness,
The twilight quietness of pose and brow.

FOR ONE BORN IN ENGLAND . . .

This was Mr. Bleaney's room . . .

—PHILIP LARKIN

For one born in England it's best to stay put,
To not travel anywhere—so the poet said—
But remain in provincial Hull, where he lived,
None of this crossing the globe at the drop of a hat.

In Hull, Birmingham, Manchester, Oxford—
I think (but don't say) this goes for London too.
A trip to Holland? You must be joking! God forbid!
What would they show you, a new dawn, the latest rainbow?

On the Continent and, what's more, having to drive on the right,
An Englishman feels uncomfortable, and a trifle odd.
And, though, speaking largely, he holds France in high regard—
Verlaine, Baudelaire, Mallarmé: a bit showy?—in their lines, their
    fates?

It is better to work one's whole life as a librarian
In a small town, exchange nods with Mr. Bleaney at the petrol pump
Or the chemist's—it's here that two words jump out—
"Hi" and "So long," we'd say in Russian.

And when the wind starts to howl at the window,
And there is exactly nowhere to go, and the mercury
Plummets, still he gets on somehow, Mr. Bleaney,
And this means you somehow manage as well.

What fortitude is needed for Venice and what ardor for Naples!
But wait, didn't Shelley dream of Italy, and Keats set out early to sail?
Yes, but when was that! Not for nothing does this world put up
So many walls, chain-linked mountains, so many barriers, borders . . .

I'd totally forgotten that we'd bought
A Christmas tree. I couldn't sleep. I went into
Another room—there it secretly scented the air
And left one Lord knows where in the backwoods.

Through forest thickets, through the thick heart
Of the woods, through the raving and torment of scorching
Coniferous heat, there in the sweet, bracing dark
It whispered to me: Don't turn on the light.

And I lowered my raised hand,
Didn't reach to turn on the overhead,
And it seemed to me I was being wrapped
In passionate embraces, and we were glad of each other.

Against the backdrop of books, chairs, chest of drawers,
In the deep darkness of the midnight hour—
Here it is, then: my love of nature,
As silly as that phrase may sound.

Heaven is where Pushkin reads Tolstoy,
Where eternal Spring springs more enticingly.
One can, of course, already imagine the meadows that bloom
Over and over—and every last sapling is green.

Besides the lush cherry trees and swelling lilacs
I like (for example) midday's sultriness too,
And the swarthy shadows of Summer evenings.
Remember the briar-rose and you'll agree.

The guests arrive at the summerhouse . . . A casual passerby
Notes the carriages clogging the seaside highway.
I don't know . . . Are all happy families alike?
I'll need to think it over . . . Not all, perhaps.

What century is it today?
Don't hurry, stand still.
The fourth, the fifth snowfall
Or, perhaps, the sixth.

It flew down to us today,
Then, after thawing, still
Showed through the way aphids do,
From under the ground.

It came down and melted,
And the old grass
Appeared again through the ice,
Without strength, barely alive.

Both a sloughed-off dream
And the faded days
Were flying like rumors
From the pursuing passersby.

It was as if last year
Were dreaming of a comeback,
As if a Gaul or Goth
Were stomping at the gate.

And when snowy sleet went over
To rain, it was as if
The Germanic chief was brushing
Sweat off his brow.

What snow there is today!
Mysterious and rich.
The fourth, the fifth century
Or, perhaps, the sixth.

My father and my mother, and all my father's
And mother's friends, and all my near and dear ones,
And all my friends—and there was no end
To this list—beyond the darkened grave
Nodding and making signs to me,
Unreadable at that distance—
I was calling them by name in my sleep
And in reality, when I woke to the dark.

The nightlight was burning, quiet reigned,
The clock did not hurry my guests,
And for the first time death was not frightening.
All of them were there, they'd made a home of it,
They had filled it up with themselves,
Its houses, flats, hallways, suites;
There too I will not be a stranger,
There too will be loved and made welcome.

Like a Roman, in general agreement with life,
You go on decently day after day,
Having marked off a lucky day with chalk
And an unlucky one with coal.

So let the calendar look like a birch trunk,
White with black marks here and there,
For tears, pain, and anger are
Necessary. How wise the Romans!

Their Stoics reflected that out of life,
At least a hundred doors lead, but into life—
Just one. Don't brood, then, do not complain—
You who are living, what's there to fear?

You can leave whenever you want,
You can step over the threshold
And starry filaments will enfold you,
A slight cosmic chill embrace you.

NOTES ON THE POEMS

For each poem, we have listed the date it was written, as supplied by the author, and the title and date of the collection in which it first appeared.

1 9 8 8 – 1 9 9 6

3 "Apollo in the Grass": Written November 11, 1989; published in *Night Music*, 1991.

5 "These days, it would be boring, to be in London, to be in Paris": Written October 5, 1987; published in *Night Music*, 1991.

6 "Nothing brings death closer for us": Written September 25, 1987; published in *Night Music*, 1991. The Russian poet Evgeny Baratynsky (1800–1844) died during a sea voyage to Sicily, never having seen Venice. The poem refers to Rembrandt's Danae painting of 1636 in the Hermitage Museum. The painting was partly destroyed by a deranged person who threw acid on it in 1985; it has since been restored.

7 "What is music?—I do not know": Written February 22, 1989; published in *Night Music*, 1991. The white hall of the poem is the main concert hall of the St. Petersburg Philharmonic.

9 "I know you, know you, have you down pat, I live in your heart": Written October 7, 1987; published in *Night Music*, 1991.

10 "Give, oh give me the purple slippers with an upgathered toe": Written September 4, 1991; published in *On a Murky Star*, 1994. "Faithful Greek woman, don't cry . . ." is an 1821 lyric of Alexander Pushkin.

12 "You will fall asleep with a lip bitten raw": Composed in the fall of 1964 when Kushner had the opportunity to send greetings to Joseph Brodsky at his place of exile in Norenskaya. Brodsky had been convicted of social par-

asitism (*tudeiadstvo*) the previous spring. The train is the one that carried Brodsky to exile, and which he later recalled in some detail: "We had a very old 'Stolypin,' a prisoner train, what's called a *vagonzak* . . . The compartment was intended to hold four, but this four-man compartment held sixteen, right? That is, the upper berth was thrown across and used like a solid ledge."* At the time of his arrest and trial Brodsky was living at his parents' apartment on Liteiny Street. The poem was first published in Talinn, Estonia, in 1990 in a collection of writings by Leningrad friends to honor Brodsky's fiftieth birthday.

*Solomon Volkov. *Conversations with Joseph Brodsky.* New York: The Free Press, 1998, p. 75.

1 3 "You, soul, *entelecheia*, as you were called": Written October 18, 1991; published in *On a Murky Star*, 1994.

1 4 "This young Rembrandt, with his feline whiskers": Written December 22, 1992; published in *On a Murky Star*, 1994. The Rembrandt self-portrait in question is the one of 1634 in the Gemäldegalerie, which Kushner saw on a visit to Berlin.

1 5 "There where it's Spring, Spring, always Spring": Written July 18, 1993; published in *On a Murky Star*, 1994.

1 6 "Dear Aleksandr, here where I write from, we have neither": Written August 26, 1989; published in *Night Music*, 1991. The letter is an imaginary one to Kushner (Aleksandr) from Brodsky (Odysseus, with whom Brodsky was often identified in Leningrad literary circles). The style of the letter also recognizably echoes Brodsky's. A pine dreaming of a palm occurs in Lermontov's poem of 1841, "In the north a pine stands alone . . . ," which is itself a translation of Heine's "Ein Fichtenbaum steht einsam." The Russian word *smuglyi* (swarthy) is a standard epithet for Pushkin.

1 8 "The only thing better than Delft in this world is this Delft on canvas": Written August 24, 1989; published in *Night Music*, 1991. The poet Evgenii Rein is a close friend who was with Kushner in Rotterdam, where the canvas of the poem, Vermeer's *View of Delft*, resides. Kushner's favorite novelist is Marcel Proust, in whose *In Search of Lost Time* the character Bergotte dies while contemplating a yellow piece of wall at an exhibit that he is viewing in preparation for an article on Vermeer. In his own essay on Vermeer, Kushner notes that Proust himself had remarked, "When I saw 'A View of Delft' in the Hague, I realized that I had seen the most beautiful painting in the world."

2 0 "It is frightening to live and, by the same token": Written December 14, 1993; published in *On a Murky Star*, 1994. Pushkin, frequently called away from his estate at Mikhailovskoe, would exit hurriedly from the porch.

2 1 "I am mistaken to say that poems take": Written September 12, 1991; published in *On a Murky Star*, 1994. Of the major Russian poets, Pushkin and Lermontov died in duels, and Mayakovsky shot himself.

2 2 "I think I know where the anguished note comes from": Written December 27, 1991; published in *On a Murky Star*, 1994. Innokenty Annensky (1856–1909) was a poet, playwright, literary critic, and translator of Euripides. Known as a poet's poet, for much of his life he taught classical languages and literatures in secondary schools. Photographs of Annensky show a proper teacher in formal dress, but what was unknown to his contemporaries was that Annensky and his stepdaughter-in-law, Olga Khmara-Barshchevskaia, fell deeply in love, although, according to her letters, the relationship remained platonic. She visited him frequently and assisted him with the publication of his manuscripts until his death.

2 3 "The Waterfall": Written June 11, 1987; published in *Night Music*, 1991. The waterfall is a classic motif in Russian nineteenth-century verse. Kushner's version is closest to Baratynsky's "Waterfall" of 1821.

2 4 "We used to write happy verses": Written February 26, 1989; published in *Night Music*, 1991. The poet and singer-songwriter Bulat Okhudzhava

(1924–1997) had a Georgian father and an Armenian mother. He is most famous for his songs set to his own poetry, which were not overtly political but whose independence was seen as a challenge by Soviet cultural authorities. Many of his songs became widely popular both in the Soviet Union and abroad. The film *There Once Lived a Song Thrush*, by the noted Georgian film director Otar Iosseliani, was a cult classic in the Soviet Union in the 1970s.

2 5 "Troy": Written November 26, 1993; published in *On a Murky Star*, 1994. The poem is dedicated to the Lithuanian poet Tomas Venclova and was inspired by a discussion they had when Kushner visited Yale, where Venclova teaches.

2 6 "In despair or in trouble, trouble": Written September 27, 1990; published in *On a Murky Star*, 1994. The line attributed to Pushkin appears in his lyric "The Desire for Fame" of 1825.

1 9 9 7 – 2 0 0 4

2 9 "If I had been born in Germany in the same year": Written June 15, 1995; published in *Millefolium*, 1998. The epigraph is a Russian proverb that appears in the poem "A Voice from the Chorus" by Aleksandr Blok, who is the "most fearless poet" of Kushner's poem.

3 0 "Do not inquire of God: He is not in this world": Written April 7, 2002; published in *Bushes*, 2002.

3 1 "Poems are anachronisms. And soon they'll disappear": Written July 31, 1994; published in *Millefolium*, 1998.

3 2 "On seeing that cottage where you and I lived": Written August 20,1998; published in *A Line of Flying Clouds*, 2000.

3 3 "If the city of Peter had been established on the Black Sea": Written November 26, 1995; published in *Millefolium*, 1998. Peter the Great captured the fortress of Azov in 1680, but it was only later, in the eighteenth century under Catherine II, that Russia reached the shores of the Black Sea.

3 4 "The Sugarbowl": Written September 29, 1995; published in *Millefolium*, 1998. Lydia Iakovlevna Ginzburg (1902–1990) was a literary critic, a student and colleague of the Russian Formalists, and one of Kushner's closest friends and mentors. In Pushkin's novel *Eugene Onegin*, Olga, the fickle younger sister of the heroine Tatyana, marries within a year of the death of her fiancé, Lensky.

3 5 "Letters": Written December 31, 1966; published in *Omens*, 1969. Although this poem appeared once in the sixties, Kushner was unable to reprint it in any of his collections until 1997. Titsian Tabidze (1895–1937), Paolo Iashvili (1895–1937), and Ilya Chavchavadze (1837–1907) were Georgian poets. Tabidze was executed and Iashvili committed suicide during the Great Terror. Chavchavadze, a champion of the late nineteenth-century Georgian independence movement, was assassinated.

3 7 "Riding into the city, you see the warehouses": Written May 31, 2002; published in *Bushes*, 2002. The Obvodny Canal is located in one of the run-down industrial areas of St. Petersburg. The abandoned train cars were the sort that used to go to the Far East, often bringing prisoners to labor camps. Pliushkin is a miser in Nikolai Gogol's novel *Dead Souls*. The verses referred to in the last stanza are from Annensky's "Oh no, it's not your figure . . ."

3 9 "I must think this through to conclusion": Written August 11, 1999; published in *A Line of Flying Clouds*, 2000. Fet's line "How pretty is the paleness . . ." is from his poem "Stay, it's fine here . . ." of 1855.

4 0 "Whether I believe in God or do not believe in god": Written August 8, 1998; published in *A Line of Flying Clouds*, 2000. Vyritsa is a summer colony about forty miles south of St. Petersburg, where Kushner has a dacha.

4 1 "Maybe this life is all one poem": Written July 12, 1996; published in *Mille-folium*, 1998.

4 2 "Farewell to the Century": Written November 6, 2001; published in *Bushes*, 2002. Andrei Ar'ev is a writer, editor, and journalist in St. Petersburg.

4 4 "I looked at the poet and thought: it's a good thing": Written February 13, 1996; published in *Millefolium*, 1998. The poem was written shortly after Kushner returned from Brodsky's funeral in New York.

4 5 "Here's what I envy: Prussian blue": Written August 13, 1998; published in *A Line of Flying Clouds*, 2000. The fourth stanza refers to Auguste Renoir's painting *Luncheon of the Boating Party*, 1881, Phillips Collection, Washington, D.C.

4 7 "When, in the end, that teacher in Poland": Written in 1966; published in *Omens*, 1969. The poem refers to Janusz Korczak, who founded a school for Jewish orphans in Warsaw and shared the fate of his students and staff who died in the Treblinka concentration camp in 1942. Nikolai Berdyaev (1874–1948) was one of the leading twentieth-century Russian Orthodox theologians.

4 8 "Venice": Written June 9, 1996; published in *Millefolium*, 1998. The gloomy genius is Baratynsky, whose estate, Muranovo, was thirty miles from Moscow. There is a sound association with the Venetian town of Murano, famous for its glass. In an epigram directed at Elisaveta Khitrovo (an aging noblewoman notorious for her bare-shouldered gowns), "Philida with each winter . . ." (1838), Baratynsky refers to her as "a sepulchral Aphrodite."

5 0 "Bushes": Written July 10, 2002; published in *Bushes*, 2002.

5 1 "A Photograph": Written June 24, 2002; published in *Bushes*, 2002. Mezhno and Pribytkovo are two small villages in the Gatchina region around Leningrad where Kushner lived with his mother in the summers before World War II.

5 7 "Evening dark brought down to nothing": Written July 12, 2009; published in *With Chalk and Coal*, 2010.

5 8 "Having overcome barriers, rises, and steps": Written September 26, 2002; published in *A Cold May*, 2005.

5 9 "Statue": Written in 1978; published in *In a New Century*, 2006.

6 0 "The garden's freshness was there in the room": Written February 26, 2004; published in *A Cold May*, 2005.

6 1 "Vesuvius preserved these frescoes for us": Written October 13, 2008; published in *With Chalk and Coal*, 2010. Irina Evsa is a poet whose work Kushner admires.

6 2 "I burned a small hole in my pants—above the knee": Written September 9, 2004; published in *A Cold May*, 2005.

6 3 "In the first century everything was supposed to end": Written June 18, 2007; published in *The Clouds Choose Anapest*, 2008.

6 4 "Can you imagine what sort of poet": Written December 6, 2004; published in *A Cold May*, 2005. Haymarket Square is a central location in Dostoevsky's *Crime and Punishment*.

6 6 "Shakespeare was mistaken to suppose": Written May 22, 2007; published in *The Clouds Choose Anapest*, 2008.

6 7 "A Little Picture Made from Blocks": Written May 27, 2009; published in *With Chalk and Coal*, 2010.

6 8 "I was standing in front of the best equestrian statue": Written October 17, 2008; published in *With Chalk and Coal*, 2010. The statue the poet admires is that of Marcus Aurelius in the Piazza del Campidoglio in Rome, which he prefers both to the ones of Italian condottieri and to the famous Falconet monument to Peter the Great, known as "The Bronze Horseman."

6 9 "For One Born in England . . .": Written June 9, 2008; published in *With*

Chalk and Coal, 2010. Kushner has spoken of his affinity with the British poet Philip Larkin. He was one of several poets who first translated Larkin into Russian.

71 "I'd totally forgotten that we'd bought": Written December 30, 2007; published in *With Chalk and Coal*, 2010.

72 "Heaven is where Pushkin reads Tolstoy": Written February 14, 2009; published in *With Chalk and Coal*, 2010. There are two references to *Anna Karenina* in the poem: the novel's famous opening sentence, and also Tolstoy's attribution of the novel's genesis to the line from an unfinished prose fragment of Pushkin's: "The guests arrived at the summerhouse . . ."

73 "What century is it today": Written January 16, 2008; published in *With Chalk and Coal*, 2010.

75 "My father and my mother, and all my father's": Written August 20, 2009; published in *With Chalk and Coal*, 2010.

76 "Like a Roman, in general agreement with life": Written February 6, 2009; published in *With Chalk and Coal*, 2010.

ACKNOWLEDGMENTS

Grateful acknowledgment is made to the following publications, where some of these translations first appeared, most in somewhat different form:

The Kenyon Review: "Apollo in the Grass"

Agni: "This young Rembrandt, with his feline whiskers"

World Literature Today: "You will fall asleep with a lip bitten raw";
"If the city of Peter had been established on the Black Sea";
"Poems are anachronisms. And soon they'll disappear"

The Anthology of Russian-Jewish Literature:
"If I had been born in Germany in the same year";
"When, in the end, that teacher in Poland"; "Letters"

Subtropics: "Here's what I envy: Prussian blue"

TRANSLATORS'

ACKNOWLEDGMENTS

We are grateful to Irina Reyfman, Alexandra Smith, and Gerald Stanton Smith for their help with elusive nuances and echoes in Kushner's poetry. Our thanks also to Jonathan Galassi for his fine ear to the English verse and sensitive editorial touch.

Aleksandr Kushner has, over many years, graciously responded to our many inquiries with answers that were modest, genuine, and genuinely helpful. We are grateful to him, above all, for the poems themselves. It has been a privilege to work with him.

We also gratefully acknowledge the National Endowment for the Arts, which supported this project with a Literary Translation Fellowship in 2003.

A Note About the Author and Translators

ALEKSANDR KUSHNER was born in Leningrad (now St. Petersburg) in 1936, and his poetry resonates with that city's rich cultural heritage. He rose to prominence as part of the post-Stalin "thaw generation," which included Andrei Bitov, Joseph Brodsky, and Evgenii Rein, and his work has reached new levels in both reputation and popularity since the breakup of the Soviet Union. His poems have been translated into more than a dozen languages and he has won virtually every national honor a Russian poet can win, and much international recognition as well.

CAROL UELAND teaches Russian language and literature at Drew University, where she directs the Russian program. Her scholarly work and translations focus on Russian poetry and Russian women's writing.

ROBERT CARNEVALE's poems have been published in *The Paris Review*, *The New Yorker*, and other magazines, as well as in anthologies. He also teaches at Drew University, in the Arts and Letters program.